WHAT EVER
HAPPENED
TO
Mary

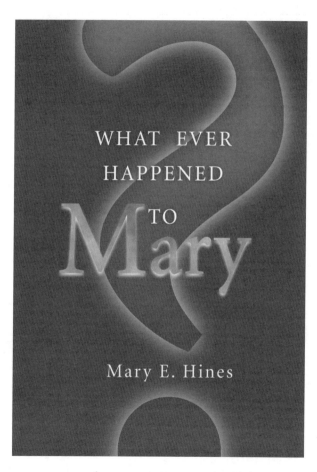

WHAT EVER

HAPPENED

TO

Mary

Mary E. Hines

ave maria press   Notre Dame, Indiana

www.avemariapress.com

International Standard Book Number: 0-87793-720-6

Cover and text design by Katherine Robinson Coleman

Printed and bound in the United States of America.

Library of Congress Cataloging-in-Publication Data
Library of Congress Cataloging-in-Publication Data
Hines, Mary E., 1943-
What ever happened to Mary? / Mary E. Hines.
        p. cm.
Includes bibliographical references.
ISBN 0-87793-720-6 (pbk.)
1. Mary, Blessed Virgin, Saint--Cult--History. 2.
Spirituality--Catholic Church--History. I. Title.
BT645 .H48 2001
232.91--dc21

                                    2001002525
                                         CIP

C O N T E N T S

	Introduction	7
CHAPTER ONE	Origins of Devotion to Mary	17
CHAPTER TWO	The Many Faces of Mary	31
CHAPTER THREE	We Fly to Thy Patronage	51
CHAPTER FOUR	New Directions	73
	Conclusion	91
	Notes	92
	Suggestions for Further Reading	93

Reflecting on the development of Catholic spirituality since the Second Vatican Council, one might be tempted to ask the question, "What ever happened to Mary?" It is generally agreed that there has been a falling off in marian devotion, at least in Europe and North America, in the years since Vatican II. Yet the figure of Mary has been central to Christian spirituality and doctrine almost from the beginning. What are the reasons for this eclipse? Is it time for a comeback of this central female figure of our tradition? Does Mary have a place in Christian spirituality of the future?

I became interested in this issue when I was teaching in a Catholic school of theology and realized that Mary had no place anywhere in the curriculum. I decided to offer a course entitled "Perspectives on Mary in Christian Tradition." At the first class meeting I was surprised to find that there were no women in the class, although there were a number in the school. In the same semester, I taught "Feminist Theology," and I found all the women! Interestingly enough, although there were many men in the school, no men had signed up for that class. (That, however, is another book entirely.) When I asked the women why they were not interested in a course on Mary, who is after all the most significant female figure in our tradition, some responded with a sense of betrayal and disillusionment, some with more a sense of undefined unease with the portrait of Mary presented to them as they were growing up. Some said that there was just too much baggage for them to summon up interest in studying Mary.

On the other hand, the men who had signed up for the class came with a variety of agendas. Some had a traditional, romantic attachment to the figure of Mary, but others—the younger among them—came out of sheer ignorance. Having grown up in a post-Vatican II church they simply knew nothing about Mary except for a vague realization that she had been very important in the faith life of their elders.

Around the same time, I had the opportunity to offer a course on Mary at one of the member schools of the ecumenical consortium in which we were involved. There I found a real interest in knowing more about Mary on the part of both women and men from a variety of Christian traditions. They were not hampered by baggage from the past and were interested in learning more about a figure who had not played an important role in their theologies or spiritualities.

These experiences—the disillusionment of many Catholic women with the traditional picture of Mary, a generation of younger Catholics who had grown up without her, as well as a newly awakened interest on the part of Protestant Christians—convinced me that we needed to get back in touch with Mary. So I began to look more deeply into this complex and fascinating figure of our faith.

Although the mother of Jesus was obviously an historical figure, she has played a symbolic role in the Christian imagination far beyond her historical roots. To say that her role has been symbolic is not to disparage it; rather it is to say that, throughout history, the figure of Mary has provided a window into the deepest truths we know about ourselves as human beings and about our God. Mary has engaged the creative minds of artists and poets, theologians and homemakers. Women and men have seen in her a model of the ideal human being, completely faithful to God's call in her life. They have suspected also that in the figure of Mary we catch a glimpse of the divine. Some of the extravagant language applied to Mary throughout history can only point to an intuition that our language about God has been impoverished by being restricted almost exclusively to male metaphors. What we were saying about Mary we wanted to be saying about God.

Devotion to Mary has remained fairly constant throughout much of Christian history since about the fourth century, with at least two notable exceptions, the Reformation and our present post-Vatican II church. The sixteenth-century reformers saw in devotion to Mary a challenge to and distraction from the exclusive worship due to God alone. As the Protestant churches developed, they increasingly marginalized the figure of Mary. In contrast, in the centuries following the Reformation, devotion to Mary became a distinguishing element of Roman Catholicism. For many of us, May processions and crownings, public rosary recitations, and the sodality were central dimensions of our Catholic childhoods. In more recent times, partly as a result of the Second Vatican Council, and partly due to changing societal and ecclesial evaluations of the role of women, devotion to Mary has again been somewhat marginalized, even in the Roman Catholic tradition.

We have learned something, though, from the experience of the Protestant churches. Something is missing when we lose touch with Mary. The figure of Mary witnesses in a symbolic way to the key role of a woman in human salvation. Protestants as well as post-Vatican II Catholics have recently begun to try to recapture the meaning of this woman so central to our faith traditions. But the excesses and problems that may have crept into past marian devotion must not be uncritically repeated in any retrieval of marian spirituality for today. For an authentic renewal in devotion to Mary the insights and concerns raised by Protestants and taken up by the Second Vatican Council must be incorporated. In addition, the experience of women today, for whom Mary is sometimes an ambiguous figure, must be taken into account in developing a renewed theology and spirituality of Mary. Many Catholic women are profoundly suspicious that the Mary tradition has been used to legitimate their secondary status in the church and in society. On the other hand, many women have found in Mary a positive image of a woman that has lent significance to lives otherwise undervalued by both church and society. Mary is indeed ambiguous.

The development of devotion to Mary followed two major paths, not always clearly distinguished. The church honored Mary by bestowing various titles on her and defining dogmas that specified and focused on certain dimensions of her privileged role in Christian history. Sometimes, but not always, connected to this there also grew a history of popular devotion which expressed Mary's deep grasp on the hearts and imaginations of those who were neither church officials nor professional theologians. Many were artists, poets, and monks. In taking another look at the Mary tradition one cannot escape the fact that the theologians, church officials, artists, poets, and monks from whom we receive both the doctrinal and devotional heritage were almost entirely men. This is not to say, necessarily, that men had greater devotion to Mary, though some would suggest this, but that men were until very recently the exclusive recorders of the tradition. Naturally, they developed and recorded a marian spirituality that reflected their experience as men, and most often as celibate men. The notable exception to this is the tradition of apparitions where women and children figure much more prominently. The great German theologian, Karl Rahner, suggested that a renewed theology of Mary will have to be developed, at least initially, by women and explicitly incorporate their experience.[1] Women have taken up this challenge. Historical and constructive works by women now explore the many facets of this intriguing figure.

In this short book we will look at some of the positive dimensions of the history of devotion to Mary—and some of the problems. Then, we will look at some of the resources for developing new approaches to Mary that include and take seriously the experience and theological reflection of women. Where traditional devotion to Mary has focused on the themes of virgin-motherhood, queenship, and intercession, this new theology and spirituality of Mary rediscovers her place in the spiritual life as our sister-disciple in the community of faith.

CHAPTER ONE

ORIGINS OF DEVOTION TO MARY

*All these were constantly devoting themselves
to prayer, together with certain women,
including Mary the mother of Jesus. . . .*

ACTS 1:14 (NRSV)

Before beginning to look at Mary's impact on our spiritual and doctrinal history it is important to review the scriptural foundations of her enormous symbolic presence in Christian tradition. The Reformation's critique of the Mary tradition, as well as the Council's critique, suggest that through the centuries marian devotion has wandered afield from its gospel beginnings. How deeply is the great queen of heaven and virgin mother rooted in the New Testament texts?

Our tradition indeed seems to tell us a great deal about Mary. We could almost be led to believe that we draw this information from an early biography or life of Mary. However, there is no biography, and historical information about this woman who is so central to our faith is surprisingly limited. Gospel references to Mary are meager. The Christian scriptures are theological documents that reflect on the ministry, mission, and redemptive significance of Jesus. Mary's role is clearly secondary to her son. We know that Mary was a young Jewish woman whom the author of the gospel of Luke identified with the lowly in society. Luke ascribes to her the *Magnificat's* powerful affirmation that the lowly will put down the mighty from their places of honor. Was she considered lowly just because she was a woman? Was she materially poor in relation to others of her time? Was she regarded as an unwed mother? Whatever the reason, the theological affirmation is that God chose a marginalized person, someone whom society would have regarded as unworthy, for a central role in human salvation.

Although the gospels contain little historical information about Mary, the theological interpretations of the different evangelists give interesting insights into how she was regarded by the early church community. The infancy narratives, although appearing to contain significant information about Mary, must be read in light of their literary genre. They reflect the early church community's later awareness of Jesus' significance and destiny. They are interested in showing that the beginnings of this remarkable figure foreshadowed his destiny. Keeping in mind, however, that the primary focus of the biblical author was not on Mary, we can reflect on the stories of the annunciation, the visitation, and the virginal conception to discover their significance for Christians today, especially women. In fact, we must do this because these vignettes have been central to the marian tradition. People have painted these vignettes, written hymns about them, and theologized about them all too often to the eventual detriment of women. We will come back to this in the chapter on marian doctrines and the spirituality encouraged by them.

Other than in the infancy stories, the mother of Jesus makes few appearances in the synoptic gospels, Mark, Matthew, and Luke. One incident is recounted by all the synoptic texts indicating that it may have a historical basis. When the family of Jesus come searching for him, Jesus comments to the disciples that his true family includes "those who hear the word of God and do it" (Lk 8:21; see also Mk 3:20-35; Mt 12:46-50). What is interesting, though, is that each of the gospel writers interprets the incident somewhat differently. Mark suggests a contrast between the biological family and the family of disciples. Surprisingly, in light of later traditions about Mary, she and the family are counted among the unbelievers who question Jesus' mission. On reflection, though, parents whose young adult children are launching careers and moving off on their own may well identify with Mary's incomprehension of her son's mission, as well as with her desire to take him home and quietly try to talk some sense into him. The gospel of Matthew weakens

Mark's negative portrayal, and Luke turns it around and pictures Mary as an example of those who hear the word of God and keep it. Since Mark is generally considered to be the earliest of the gospels, this may reflect a development in light of Mary's later significant role in the post-resurrection community. It may also reveal that, like all of us, Mary grew in her understanding of her own vocation and that of her son. Luke's positive interpretation may foreshadow Acts 1:14 where Mary is pictured among the disciples gathered in the upper room at pentecost. Her faith journey led to a privileged role in the early Christian community. Since pentecost has been traditionally considered the foundation event of the church, this image of Mary among the disciples has grounded early and more recent interpretations of Mary as Mother of the church or model of Christian discipleship.

Two texts from the gospel of John which have captured Christian imagination and strongly influenced the development of marian spirituality are the wedding feast at Cana (Jn 2:1-12) and the image of Mary at the foot of the cross (Jn 19:25-27). These texts have quite different consequences. The wedding feast has led to imaging Mary as intercessor and mediator with her sometimes reluctant son. This theme of intercession became central to the Mary tradition as it developed through the centuries, with some problematic consequences. The scene at the foot of the cross is a discipleship image once again portraying Mary as a model of belief and discipleship, the consummate member of the believing community.

Paul never mentions Mary by name, affirming only that Jesus was "born of a woman." He does not seem to know of the infancy stories and his concern in making his affirmation appears to be to underline the true humanity of Jesus.

This is the basic information about Mary contained in the New Testament as we know it today. Mary remains a somewhat shadowy figure whose life as a young Jewish woman was dramatically altered by God's challenging invitation.

The other important source of traditions about Mary is the Infancy Gospel of James. Although not included in the scriptures with which we are familiar, this gospel serves as the source for much of the "biographical" information thought to be known about Mary and has had considerable influence, especially in popular devotion to Mary. Prior to Vatican II, when Catholics rarely read the Bible for themselves, most Catholics probably assumed that this information was indeed contained in the New Testament. The style of the gospel of James is similar to the infancy narratives of the synoptic gospels, although much more fanciful and much more interested in Mary in her own right. It recounts the circumstances of Mary's birth to a rich man named Joachim and his wife Anna. Just as the traditional gospels focused on the remarkable dimensions of Jesus' birth in light of his later destiny, the second-century gospel of

James tells the story of the birth of Mary in strikingly similar terms, terms often drawn from the Jewish scriptures such as the story of Abraham and Sarah. The childlessness of Sarah and her miraculous conception in old age closely parallels the story of Anna: "Suddenly a messenger of the Lord appeared to her and said: 'Anna, Anna, the Lord God has heard your prayer. You will conceive and give birth, and your child will be talked about all over the world'" (InJas 4:1). Surely a prediction which has come true!

Other legends familiar to most Catholics come from the Infancy Gospel of James, such as the miraculous staff of Joseph indicating he was to be Mary's protector, the image of Joseph as an old man, and the centrality of Mary's virginity, beginning with her (historically unlikely) dedication as a virgin in the Temple at age three. As a second-century document, this gospel reflects the cultural value that some elements of the society of the time placed on abstinence, self-denial, and virginity. Not only is

Mary pictured as a virgin before the birth of Jesus, but James insists that she remained a virgin even during and after the birth. This emphasis on Mary's virginity became a central motif of further marian development and was one influence on the second class status often attributed to married women in Christian tradition, and to the unhealthy denigration of sexuality as a spiritual reality. Virginity became equated with spirituality so that married women often had difficulty understanding themselves as having a spirituality that grew out of their experience as married women.

The meager information presented in the traditional gospels and the more legendary narrative of James are the foundations upon which all later theology of Mary has been built. It is important to start our reflections here to remind ourselves of the modest historical base on which this tradition has been constructed. Even in the early centuries of the church, the symbolic meaning of Mary had begun to develop far beyond historical knowledge. This is not necessarily a negative phenomenon, but it is important to keep in mind the biblical picture of the young Jewish woman who actively and courageously responded to God's initiative in her life. This can serve as a historical point of reference and a reality check against which to evaluate later development in theology, images, and devotion to Mary.

Questions for Reflection & Discussion

1. *The following are New Testament texts that include some reference to Mary. One way to appreciate these texts is to read and reflect on them as a whole to gain a perspective on how Mary and her role were understood and appreciated by the early Christian community that was the source for the texts.*

   Another approach would be to read each text separately and to reflect and pray about it.

   Events surrounding the birth of Jesus:
   Matthew 1:1-2:23
   Luke 1:5-2:52

Mary during the public ministry of Jesus:
Mark 3:20-35
Matthew 12:46-50
Luke 8:19-21; 11:27-28

Mary in the gospel of John:
John 2: 1-12
John 19: 25-27

Mary and the church:
Acts 1:14

2. *Which episode in Mary's life has played a central role in your awareness of her? Can you think of reasons why it is so significant?*

3. *What themes about Mary emerge as you reflect on the scriptural portrait of her? Are these the themes that have been central in your own awareness of her role?*

4. *What themes in these scriptures speak most strongly to you about your own life and faith?*

CHAPTER TWO

THE
MANY
FACES
OF
MARY

It is fitting that the Virgin should be resplendent with a purity such that none could be conceived more perfect save only God's.

ANSELM, *DE CONCEPTU VIRGINALI*, CAP. XVIII

Therefore she is also hailed as a pre-eminent and altogether singular member of the Church, and as the Church's model and excellent exemplar in faith and charity.

VATICAN II, *CONSTITUTION ON THE CHURCH*, PARA. 53

In this chapter we will look at what the official church has taught about Mary through bestowing titles on her and defining dogmas about her. We can only touch on some of the most central of these titles and dogmas, paying particular attention to how they have translated into attitudes and expectations of women.

The early church drew parallels between Mary and Eve. While Eve was depicted as the one through whom sin came into the world, Mary, the "new Eve" was the vehicle of salvation. One problem with this typology was that it laid the blame for sin squarely at the feet of women, who became regarded as seductive temptresses. While Mary was also a woman, doctrines that focused on her perfect virginity and divine motherhood tended to remove her from the experience of real women. It is worth reflecting, at least briefly, on the central faith affirmations of Mary as virgin and mother and their impact on Christian spirituality and on the lives of women.

Mary Ever Virgin

As mentioned already, emphasis on Mary's virginity in many ways reflected the ascetic ideals of much of the second-century world. While there is reference in Luke's gospel to the virginal conception of Jesus, the doctrines of the virgin birth and the perpetual virginity came into the church's teaching in the second century as a reflection of the growing interest in Mary. In the philosophical and religious climate of the second century, it was unimaginable to think that this pure virgin could have been sullied by any experience of human sexuality. While, within the context of the time, this was perhaps an understandable way for the church to express its esteem for the mother of the Savior, the consequences this has had for the church's attitude to women and to sexuality and marriage are troubling. This becomes especially problematic when coupled with an understanding of Eve as responsible for the fallen state of humanity, and women as complicit in the seduction which led to human sinfulness. No wonder women through the ages have suffered the consequences of this negative evaluation.

In interpreting these doctrines it is important to remember that the early church did not delve into the biology of these affirmations.

They were statements of faith intended to high-light the enormous significance of the person and mission of Jesus, the Christ in terms that would have been meaningful to people of the time. Later Christians became more interested in the biological workings of these statements and these became understood as part of the doctrine. Just as in biblical interpretation, in understanding church doctrine one must look carefully for the faith statement which the church intends to be held for all time and distinguish that from other elements which are necessary to make such a statement within a particular worldview. There is no denying that our worldview has changed dramatically from the second century. There is also no doubt that our scientific knowledge has advanced since then. In light of today's knowledge and experience, for some women and men, the tradition of Mary's perpetual virginity has become an obstacle to faith rather than a window into the mystery of God. While the official church has through history presupposed Mary's virginity to be a historical and biological reality and continues to do so today, it may be more helpful for many contemporary Catholics to focus more on the theological meaning of this church tradition. What can the tradition of Mary's virginity say to us today?

Because of the problematic way these dogmas have been interpreted, leading to a negative view of human sexuality and creating an impossible ideal for most women who are sexually active, many women may not choose to focus on these dogmas as elements of their spirituality. As Karl Rahner suggests, they may wish to focus on more central dimensions of faith as paths into the incomprehensible mystery.[2]

For others, however, the symbol of the virginity of Mary may continue to function as a protest against the physical exploitation of women. Advocates of liberation mariology suggest that Mary's virginity can serve as a symbol of women's freedom from unhealthy dependence on men particularly in countries where women remain subservient in economic and sexual areas. Within such a worldview, reflection on Mary's virginity may offer women the freedom to actualize their solidarity with the poor and oppressed of society.

Mary, Mother of God and Our Mother

Devotion to Mary's motherhood received great impetus from the proclamation of Mary as *Theotokos*, "God-bearer," at the Council of Ephesus in 431. From that time, Christians were able to venerate Mary not only as Mother of Jesus but as Mother of God. Not surprisingly, it was in this city of Diana, goddess of the Ephesians, that devotion to Mary began the trajectory which so focused on Mary's unique privileges as to almost place her on a level with God's own self, a sort of universal mother to humanity—almost a goddess, perhaps taking the place of the goddesses of old. Mary, Mother of God was soon venerated in Christian spirituality as our Mother, just as God was seen as our Father. Although the church's doctrinal tradition counseled against worship of Mary as equal to God, popular devotion often came close to crossing this line. In a later chapter we will look at some of the reasons why Christians might have turned to Mary as equal and sometimes more powerful than God. In the next chapter we will look more carefully at the development of the tradition of prayer to Mary, which followed on this major marian title.

Mary Immaculate

The privilege-centered mariology that followed from seeing Mary as mysteriously both virgin and mother culminated in the two great dogmas of the Assumption and the Immaculate Conception, the definitions of which framed one of the periods of most intense marian devotion in the church's history. The Immaculate Conception was defined in 1854 by papal pronouncement, anticipating the dogma of papal infallibility adopted at the First Vatican Council. The Assumption was similarly defined in 1950. Although the Assumption had been an object of belief rather consistently through history, the Immaculate Conception had a more checkered history. Thomas Aquinas, for one, had serious reservations about whether belief in the Immaculate Conception challenged belief in the universal need for redemption by Christ. Nevertheless, by 1854 a general consensus of Catholics supported Pius IX's definition of the Immaculate Conception as a matter of faith, and the same was true when Pius XII defined the Assumption. These definitions seemed to seal the church's veneration of Mary as privileged beyond all other human beings, "alone of all her sex," or in the words of the nineteenth-century poet William Wordsworth, "our tainted nature's solitary boast" (from "Sonnet to the Virgin").

Understanding Mary as exempt from the tendency to sinfulness, which experience tells us is the common human lot, and as dispensed from the bodily corruption which is our universal fate, created an ambiguous situation. On the one hand, a woman was a central and powerful icon in the Roman Catholic tradition. A female figure occupied a place second only to God doctrinally and her figure played a powerful role in the Catholic devotional imagination. On the other hand, it is ironic that having a woman so central to the tradition has often not translated into respect and equality for women in Roman Catholicism. The primary conveyers of the Mary tradition were celibate males who tended to create a romanticized, ideal woman high on a pedestal and out of the reach of real women who were more often associated with the seductive temptress, Eve. Protestantism had largely rejected any devotion to Mary as interposing a mediator between God and the one mediator, Jesus Christ. Though they were on theologically correct ground, this rejection of Mary led in these traditions to a religious tradition one-sidedly masculine in its images and symbols. This was the situation until Vatican II set the church on a new direction.

A New Theological Approach

A shift away from this privilege-centered mariology began in the first half of the twentieth century which eventually culminated in a new approach to Mary taken by the Second Vatican Council. This began with a new way of interpreting the two modern marian dogmas. The theology of Karl Rahner typifies this approach. Rahner was concerned that people of the twentieth century would find the dogmas of faith unbelievable, obstacles rather than aids to faith. He felt that unless it could be demonstrated that there was a connection between people's experience and the church's dogmas they would not be able to play a living role in their spiritual lives and would become increasingly irrelevant for contemporary Christians.

Rahner looked for this connection by interpreting the Immaculate Conception and the Assumption not as completely unique privileges of Mary alone but as representative of all human life. These two dogmas, having to do with the beginning and end of Mary's life, affirm that her whole life was caught up in God's grace. The Immaculate Conception implies that, in virtue of the redeeming action of her son, Mary was graced from the first moment of her conception. Much contemporary Catholic theology would affirm this of us all. God offers God's own life to each and every human being from the very beginning of life. Our lives are a process of acceptance of that offer. The Assumption affirms that body and soul, Mary's whole person is with God, her life accepted and validated by God. She accepted God's love and responded totally in full human freedom. It is our hope that our lives too will be freely responsive to God's initiative and find God's ultimate gracious acceptance as Mary did (see Rahner's *Mary: Mother of the Lord*). This interpretation sees Mary not as uniquely privileged, apart from other human beings, but as one of us who has gone before us and shows us the way.

Building on this, Vatican Council II made a major shift in Catholic understanding of Mary. Coming as it did at a peak moment in marian devotion, about ten years after the definition of the Assumption, one might have expected more definitions and titles. Some wanted a definition of Mary as mediatrix of all graces or even as co-redemptrix. Some council fathers wanted to devote a whole document to her. There was indeed a great debate at the council between those who wanted mariology to continue in its traditional directions and those who thought there was need of a correction in course. Ultimately, the second group won out. Rather than a document devoted to Mary herself, the material on Mary was included as chapter eight within the Dogmatic Constitution on the Church, *Lumen Gentium*.[3] This signaled a new direction in theology of Mary where she is seen as a model of discipleship *within* the community of believers. The reasons for this shift are important in understanding the role of Mary since the time of the council.

There was a concern that abuses had crept into the marian tradition over the years, which perhaps lent credence to the Protestant critique of exaggeration and even superstition in Catholic devotion to Mary. The ecumenical atmosphere of the Second Vatican Council led it to reassert clearly the orthodox belief that there is only one mediator, Jesus, the Christ. Mary is clearly positioned on the human side of the human/divine equation. Mary is seen primarily as a woman of faith who freely responded to God's call in her life. Her physical motherhood is contextualized within her role as faithful disciple. This understanding of Mary's role calls into question the church's curious tendency on the one hand to exalt virginity as the highest calling and at the same time to assert repeatedly in church and papal documents that motherhood is the role most appropriate for the essential nature of women. Such language serves to marginalize both those women who choose the single life and those who choose to become mothers. If we took seriously the council's approach, then the call to ministry and discipleship would be the center for all Christians, with the call to marriage, the single life, or celibate religious community among the appropriate contexts for an individual to fulfill this fundamental call.

Vatican Council II, then, signaled a shift away from a privilege-centered mariology and stressed continuities between Mary and all those called to discipleship within the Christian community. Mary is our sister in the faith, the one who has gone before us and shows us the way. She is the faithful disciple who has finished the journey and kept the faith. She is type and model of the church. Mary is thus an example for all Christians, not just for women. Oftentimes the biblical story of the annunciation, Mary's fiat to God's will for her, had been interpreted as an example of the posture considered appropriate for women in the church: receptive, meek, and acquiescent. In the light of Vatican II and more recent biblical scholarship, a more adequate interpretation would recognize that Mary freely chose her involvement in God's plan by responding with a yes to God's call, and not without some theological discussion, as is indicated in the dialogue with the angel in the annunciation story. Far from passive, hers was an active role and serves as a model for all Christians—women and men—in discerning how best to actualize their call to discipleship.

After Vatican II there was not the immediate renewal in theology of Mary and the spirituality that flows from it that might have been expected. In western Europe and North America, Mary largely disappeared from the Catholic scene. It was felt by many that Mary represented a secondary level of Catholic doctrine, and attention after the council focused on renewal in what were considered the more central areas of liturgy, theology of church, and eventually Christology. Little new theology of Mary was produced in the twenty-five years following the council and many young Catholics grew up aware of devotion to Mary only as a historical curiosity of the Catholicism of their parents and grandparents. The study of mariology in itself disappeared from theology departments and seminaries and oddly enough did not reappear in the study of church (ecclesiology), as might have been expected in light of conciliar theology. In countries where marian devotion continued, it was little influenced by the new directions of the council.

Only since the mid-eighties has there been a reawakening of interest in Mary largely initiated by the new phenomenon of women theologians, as well as liberation theologians, from all over the world. Although acknowledging the ambiguities of the Mary tradition, these theologians point out the loss that is incurred in the eclipse of this central female figure. Mary herself, they say, needs to be liberated from the idealized projections of past portrayals and the superstition which sometimes marred authentic devotion to this mysterious Jewish woman.

These new theologies of Mary build on the Vatican II picture of Mary as companion disciple and sister in faith. We will examine more closely some of these new directions, but first we will look briefly at the history of devotion to Mary and try to get at some of the reasons for an apparent widespread diminishment in what was once such a central dimension of Catholic life and spirituality.

Questions for Reflection & Discussion

1. *How has the church's emphasis on Mary's virginity affected your appreciation of her? Has it had any impact on your own spirituality? In what ways?*

2. *Has the characterization of Mary as "alone of all her sex" or as "our tainted nature's solitary boast" been significant in your awareness of her?*

   Are there ways in which a focus on Mary's uniqueness might be helpful to you?

   Are there ways in which it would be unhelpful?

3. *Are there titles or doctrines about Mary that have been central to your awareness and understanding of Mary? Have these changed over time in relation to your own spiritual journey?*

4. *Reflect on the theologian Karl Rahner's interpretation of the dogmas of the Immaculate Conception and the Assumption. Does his insight (these dogmas imply that all of our lives, from beginning to end, are caught up in God's grace) offer you new ways to relate to Mary?*

CHAPTER THREE

We Fly
to
Thy
Patronage

We fly to thy patronage,
O holy Mother of God!
Despise not our petitions in our necessities,
but deliver us from all dangers,
O ever glorious and blessed Virgin.

This ancient prayer, *Sub tuum praesidium*, is an early example of Christians turning to Mary in prayer, asking for her favor and her intercession with God. It marks the beginning of a very central motif in Christian tradition—looking to Mary for help in meeting the many difficulties of life. Unlike the doctrinal tradition discussed in Chapter Two, which was primarily a phenomenon of the official church, devotion to Mary in large part grew up among the people. While the doctrinal tradition makes Mary's virginity and purity central, popular devotion turned to Mary as mother to humanity, or perhaps more as today's indulgent grandmother. In this popular tradition, Mary is not often assigned the disciplinary function common to parents but rather is the one who stays the hand of the stern father-God. She also becomes a sort of substitute mediator for her son who is imaged as a justice-minded judge able to be swayed by the merciful intercession of his mother.

Prayers, litanies, and poetry characteristic of each particular historical period's view of Mary (and of women in general) expressed the deep devotion of Christians to this ideal woman. They sometimes, however, slipped over the edge and attributed to Mary power and activity more properly belonging to God alone. Perhaps unconsciously too, this kind of devotion to Mary reinforced an idea of Jesus as a distant and punitive judge. People began to feel that they needed a mediator or intercessor with Jesus who, in the popular mind, lost his role as the one and only mediator between God and humankind.

Throughout history there were periods of more or less intense devotion to Mary, but a particularly intense period just preceded the Second Vatican Council. This modern period roughly coincided with the years between the definition of the Immaculate Conception in 1854 and the Assumption in 1950. The definition of the Immaculate Conception celebrated in an official way the deep devotion of Catholics to Mary who was regarded as mother, queen, and the ideal of Catholic womanhood. Catholic spirituality in this period included in a very central way May processions, devotions like the May altar, sodalities, exhortations to be "Marylike," and family recitations of the rosary. Catholics were exhorted always to go "to Jesus through Mary." The Litany of Loreto that called on Mary as Ark of the Covenant and House of Gold was a familiar prayer and the *Memorare* epitomized many Catholics' faith in Mary's intercessory power.

> Remember, O most gracious Virgin Mary, that never was it known

that anyone who fled to thy protection, implored thy help, and sought thy intercession, was left unaided. Inspired with this confidence, I fly unto thee, O Virgin of virgins, my Mother! To thee I come; before thee I stand, sinful and sorrowful. O Mother of the Word Incarnate, despise not my petitions, but in thy mercy, hear and answer me. Amen.

Catholics turned to Mary for protection and stability, in particular, during the first half of the twentieth century, marked as it was by two world wars and the threat of communism. She provided a peaceful beacon of hope and security in this threatening and changing world.

Many Catholics focused their devotion to Mary on the sites of marian apparitions. Lourdes and Fatima were centers of great devotion and pilgrimage. The message of the apparitions often fit into the worldview of the times, calling for repentance and conversion so that Mary could stay the hand of a Jesus who threatened calamitous destruction in this world and perhaps eternal damnation. This fearful view perhaps reflected the anxieties of modern Catholics confronting the new and destructive possibilities of nuclear weapons.

I think that it is fair to say that Mary plays a less significant role in Catholic spirituality today. Of course generalizations are dangerous, but it seems that many Catholics who took seriously the new directions of Vatican II found Mary becoming less and less central to their spiritual lives. For some, this was almost unconscious and it is only now, thirty years later, that they begin to ask the question, "What ever happened to Mary?" Although some Catholics continued to have deep devotion to Mary, I think there has been a dramatic decline in the centrality of Mary in Catholic spiritual life. It is worth looking at some of the causes for this decline, what some of the positive values of this devotion were, some of the negatives, and some directions for the future which preserve the positive and avoid the negative.

The impact of Vatican II on the theology of Mary has already been mentioned. In addition to this, at least four other influences have shaped the way many present-day Catholics view Mary: the effect of the biblical renewal (with the recovery of a more compassionate image of the human Jesus), the ecumenical movement, the liturgical movement, and the feminist movement.

The Biblical Renewal

Chapter One discussed the biblical portrait of Mary as it emerges from the pages of the New Testament, but the biblical renewal also opened the way for new insights into Jesus himself. This changed understanding of Jesus has had a critical impact on the role Mary is seen to play in the Christian life. Simply put, the twentieth century has placed major emphasis on the recovery of the human Jesus. Jesus' humanity shows us the face of God. Although the Council of Chalcedon in 451 declared that Jesus was truly human and truly divine, popular

Christianity through the years has often seen Jesus primarily as divine, only thinly disguised as a human being. Christologies have focused on the birth and the death and resurrection of Jesus as the key moments of his salvific work. More recent Christologies, however, have tried to balance this picture by recovering the life and ministry of Jesus, or the story of Jesus. This scholarly work has coincided with the actual experience of many Catholics reading the New Testament themselves, often for the first time, and finding there a picture of the compassionate Jesus who heals the sick, associates with those thought undesirable by the society of the time, tax collectors, women, lepers. . . . This is not the judging, vengeful Christ from whom we need to be protected by the mitigating intervention of his mother. This is a Jesus who is already on our side, who shows us that God does not stand poised to punish but rather reaches out to us to pick us up when we fall.

The recovery of the human Jesus called into question for many the traditional role of

Mary as intercessor. If Jesus is infinitely approachable himself, why go through Mary? For many Catholics, the period after Vatican II was a time to recover, or discover, a deep and personal relationship with Jesus as friend and inspiration for life's journey. Mary gradually slipped out of the picture.

The Liturgical Movement

A second, and related, reason for Mary's gradual overshadowing came from the liturgical theology which preceded and followed Vatican II. The liturgical movement was committed to restoring the centrality of the eucharistic liturgy as the source and summit of Catholic spiritual life. Liturgists were concerned about practices like saying the rosary during Mass and the predominance of processions and litanies to Mary in the lives of many Catholics. They were concerned that some Catholics seemed to place more importance on their individual devotion to Mary than to communal participation in the eucharist. They feared that, for some, marian practices such as novenas and first Saturday devotions bordered on the superstitious, seeming to give Mary power to manipulate God into doing her will.

The Constitution on the Sacred Liturgy of Vatican II (*Sacrosanctum Concilium*) reminded Catholics that "the liturgy is thus the outstanding means by which the faithful can express in their lives, and manifest to others, the mystery of Christ and the real nature of the true Church"(SC, para. 2). Although the council did say that there remained a place for the popular devotions of the people, the main effort following the council went to reforming the liturgy itself so that there was more room for participation by the people and its communal dimensions became more evident. With this focus on the eucharist as the center of Catholic life, Mary once again was sidelined. Public devotions to Mary, once a principal feature of parish life, became much rarer. Where they continued to exist, fewer and fewer parishioners participated.

The Ecumenical Movement

A third influence on the decline of devotion to Mary was the ecumenical movement. In addition to the official ecumenism witnessed to by the ongoing dialogues among the Christian churches, there exists a popular ecumenism. This popular ecumenism results from the increased contacts among Roman Catholics and members of other Christian traditions. In this day to day contact, the perceptions of other Christians about Catholic devotion to Mary are revealed. Protestant Christians often see devotion to Mary as taking away from the focus on Christ as the sole mediator between God and humanity. They are suspicious of what they see as Catholic excess in devotion to Mary, who is, after all, a human being like ourselves. They are rightly suspicious of any appearance of being able to manipulate God. Vatican II was sensitive to these critiques and recognized the insights of the Protestant churches as a helpful critique of the Roman Catholic church, also always in need of reformation and renewal. Especially in the pluralistic religious culture of North America, with increased and positive contact with other Christian traditions, these insights from their Protestant neighbors also affected the spirituality of Catholics. This was yet another reason for Mary's decline.

The Feminist Movement

A fourth influence leading to this lessening of concentration on Mary came from the women's movement. The beginning of an enormous shift in society's expectations of women and in women's expectations of and for themselves coincided with Vatican Council II. Sometimes referred to as the second wave of feminism (the first wave considered to have culminated with the winning of the vote for women in 1920), women began to look outside the home, as well as within, for a place to contribute their diverse gifts and talents. They pointed to the double standard that made women permanent second class citizens, barred from certain occupations because of their sex, and often paid less for rendering the same services in areas where they were permitted to work.

Let me stop for a moment and explain my use of the term "feminist" or "feminism." Feminism is a broad movement including people of diverse positions on individual issues. It is sometimes erroneously identified exclusively with one or another of these positions and thus some people become suspicious of the term. I use it here consciously in a broad sense to mean a movement which stands for the fundamental equality of all human beings and which holds that no one should be excluded from exercising one's gifts and talents solely on the basis of sex. I also take it to mean a recognition that, historically, women have not been regarded as equals so that in making the affirmation that all persons are equal one must specify that this includes women.

Societal feminism's broadening of the arena for women's contribution of course impacted women's understandings of their role in the church. Women began to recognize that not only were they second class citizens in the world, but they were also marginalized in the church. Even worse, as I mentioned earlier, many women began to suspect that the traditional image of Mary had played a key role in their oppression. The prevalent marian image of the sweetly submissive maiden, presented as the ideal woman, seemed to many to be the religious foundation for their subordinate role. The kind of mariology which focused on Mary's privileges seemed to set her apart from other women, an ideal, but an ideal impossible for real women to attain. What real woman can be both virgin and mother? Mary was placed on a pedestal, admired, but out of the reach of ordinary women.

Medieval writers had extolled Mary as the great queen of heaven; distant, beautiful, and powerful. This queenly image represented the ideal of womanhood at the time. Crusaders carried her beautiful image into battle. Some of the most well known and loved marian anthems are composed to Mary as queen, the *Salve Regina*, for example:

> Hail, holy Queen, Mother of Mercy, our life, our sweetness, and our hope.
>
> To thee do we cry, poor banished children of Eve.
>
> To thee do we send up our sighs, mourning and weeping in this valley of tears.
>
> Turn then, most gracious advocate, thine eyes of mercy toward us;
>
> and after this our exile, show us unto the blessed fruit of they womb, Jesus.
>
> O clement, O loving, O sweet Virgin Mary.

Early twentieth century writers tried to recapture a more down to earth, human Mary. In doing so, they viewed Mary through the lens of the ideal woman of their own period, putting her on a different kind of pedestal. She was silent, compliant, humble, and uncomplaining. Rather than exercising the public power of queenship, the Mary of the early twentieth century exercised her influence behind the scenes. She was the ideal mother and housewife in an ideal nuclear family.

The extended narrative poem, "A Woman Wrapped in Silence," written in 1941 by John W. Lynch, was very influential on people's perceptions of Mary in the 1950s and early 1960s. Mary is pictured as silent, inner-directed and receptive, reliant on the strong protection and understanding of Joseph, who plays a large role in the narrative. Lynch writes of Mary:

> The heart that holds great gifts
> within itself
> Keeps silence, and it does not whisper
> on
> Of secret satisfactions, nor peruse
> Its triumphs in a hid complacency.[4]

This image of Mary is very much what society of the time expected of women so it is not surprising that it found a resonance both with women and men. The problem was that it reinforced a certain stereotyped understanding of qualities and behaviors appropriate to women. Women's talents were seen as most suited to the private sector of life, as mentioned above, not necessarily powerless, but powerful *behind* the scenes—training men for the public roles they would be called to play. Of Mary's life in Nazareth, Lynch writes:

> It is a summary a man might make
> Within a phrase, who had been
>   hearing only
> Of simplicities, the one brief word
> That could be written after he had
>   harked
> In wonder to the long sweet counting
>   over
> Of her days, and to the unaffected
> Telling that they ran so gently on

That no sign came of them, nor
    dominance
Beyond the manner of all homes
    where young
Sons are who wait for stature and
    give strong
Obedience.[5]

With the advent of the women's movement this stereotypical view of women's role began to be seriously challenged. And many women began to question the image of Mary that had been used to promote these virtues as particular to women.

Many women of that period would testify that this image of Mary served to lend dignity and inspiration to their lives. One woman, for example, remarked to me that devotion to Mary was what enabled her to get through the day as a homemaker in the 1950s. However, by the late 1960s a certain disillusionment was setting in and many women began to suspect that Mary was being used to keep women satisfied with a very secondary place in the church and world. For some women, this led to a deliberate rejection of Mary as part of their spirituality; for others, this newly awakened consciousness, combined with the impact of the other influences I have already mentioned, led to a more subtle and gradual moving away from Mary as a central figure in their lives.

For all these reasons, the theology of Vatican II, the biblical renewal, the ecumenical movement, and feminism, Mary seemed to disappear not only from Catholic theology but also from Catholic spirituality in a rather dramatic way in the years following Vatican II.

In the last ten years or so however, there has been a renaissance of interest in Mary coming from a number of directions. Courses on Mary are reappearing in seminaries, often taught by women, new theological works are being written, many by women, and Mary has been the subject of significant ecumenical dialogue. These new approaches build on the insights from Vatican II theology, ecumenical perspectives, liturgical and biblical studies, and especially the experience of women. They offer new insights into Mary, remaining faithful to the New Testament but offering inspiration to women and men today in the struggle to live Christian lives in our challenging contemporary world. Chapter Four will focus on some of these new directions.

Questions for Reflection & Discussion

1. Has Mary's role as intercessor been central to your awareness of her?

2. Are there particular prayers or devotions to Mary that have been meaningful to your faith life and spirituality?

3. Do you feel that it is important to go "to Jesus through Mary"?

4. Has your awareness of Mary been affected by contact with Protestant Christians?

5. In your experience, has the image of Mary affected attitudes toward women in the church?

CHAPTER FOUR

New
DIRECTIONS

. . . Mary, the valiant and prophetic daughter of Sion, committed to justice, faithful to her God and to her people, inspires and strengthens women's unity and struggle, redeeming and ennobling them in their own eyes.[6]

MARÍA CLARA BINGEMER

One resource for getting back in touch with Mary comes from the official church in the apostolic exhortation of Pope Paul VI, *Marialis Cultus*, which develops guidelines for a post-Vatican II renewal of popular devotion to Mary. *Marialis Cultus* responds to a significant omission in the Vatican II treatment of Mary. Where Vatican II critiqued some past marian practices as exaggerations, superstitions, or substitutions for the church's liturgy, it did not provide any positive new approaches to reclaiming this tradition in a more constructive way. Emphasis on the eucharist as the center of the church's worship seemed to leave little room for devotion to Mary. Many will remember the post-Vatican II period as a time when statues disappeared overnight to allow a central focus on the altar. Some will also have noticed that, of late, the statues have been creeping back in. This is part of a rethinking of the value of popular devotions, such as the devotions to Mary. Yes, there were excesses and misdirections, but there were also positive values in this tradition. One value that immediately springs to mind is that marian devotions could be led by laity and often centered in the home. The unintended result of their cessation was that Catholic ritual became even more dependent on clergy and centered in the sanctuary. Popular devotions reflected a sense of ownership among the laity and often expressed deep religious convictions.

Paul VI's *Marialis Cultus* offers the guidelines for a renewal of popular devotion that were missing from Vatican II. It tries to retrieve the values of traditional devotion to Mary within guidelines that reflect the emphases of Vatican II. Paul VI recognizes the need for dialogue with the social and cultural climate of the time in developing new expressions of marian spirituality. "Certain practices of piety that not long ago seemed suitable for expressing the religious sentiment of individuals and of Christian communities seem today inadequate or unsuitable because they are linked with social and cultural patterns of the past."[7] He goes on to say that the changed reality of women in society is a phenomenon that must be considered in any renewal of marian devotion. Four principles, he suggests, should guide this renewal. First, marian devotion should be rooted in the biblical texts and reflect the fundamental themes of the Christian message. Second, marian devotion should harmonize, but not merge with or replace the liturgy: it should be inspired by the liturgy and lead toward it. Third, renewed marian devotion should be ecumenically sensitive, avoiding misleading exaggeration. Fourth, Pope

Paul VI explicitly recognizes that the changed situation of women in society can cause them to be alienated from images of Mary which glorify a restricted and passive role for women. He suggests that the gospels themselves offer other images more suitable for today's women and men; for example, Mary as the first and most perfect of Jesus' disciples, who heard the word of God and acted on it; as a strong woman who experienced poverty and suffering, flight and exile; and as a spokesperson for the poor and oppressed of society. These guidelines from *Marialis Cultus* are an important impetus toward a responsible renewal of marian spirituality in the post-conciliar period.

Apparitions

In this context, I might mention marian apparitions as a dimension of popular devotion to Mary that are once again drawing the attention of some Catholic people. Lourdes, Fatima, and Guadalupe have been consistent places of pilgrimage, and recently the apparitions at

Medjugorje have been attracting attention. People often ask what the official church's attitude is about these appearances. One point of reference would be Paul VI's guidelines. In addition, the American bishops in their pastoral letter, *Behold Your Mother*, explain the church's official position. The current practice of the church is to investigate thoroughly such phenomena. When the church approves an apparition for private devotion, which it has done in relatively few cases (for example, Lourdes and Fatima), it certifies that it involves nothing contrary to faith and morals and that it supports the public revelation of the gospel, which is always the norm. The Vatican has been cautious in its approach to Medjugorje which has, to this point, not received official church approval. Those apparitions which have received church approval *may* become part of the devotional life of Catholics, but are never obligatory.[8]

In the light of the church's explicit recognition of its social mission to transform structures of injustice in the world, some question the privatistic and conservative messages of many of the marian apparitions. Others, however, suggest that these phenomena are more complex. The messages of the marian apparitions, they say, have most often been entrusted to the poor and marginalized of society. Our Lady of Guadalupe in particular has been a powerful symbol of liberation for an oppressed people. One touchstone for evaluating the impact of devotion to particular apparitions on one's spirituality might be whether one is led to deepen one's spiritual life, both in terms of love of God and service to others. An excessively inwardly focused spirituality or emphasis on the unusual and spectacular does not reflect the gospel witness that the church regards as the mark of an apparition's authenticity.

Building on, and compatible with the directions of Vatican II and these official guidelines, important new insights into Mary are also coming from the experience and work of liberation and feminist theologians.

Mary Rediscovered

Liberation theologies arise out of the situation of the oppressed and marginalized of society. These theologies, which first appeared in Latin America in the 1970s, take as a starting point the struggle for the kind of social change that will bring about a more just world for all. In Mary, liberation theology has found a potent symbol for this struggle. Her prophetic role in the *Magnificat* as the spokesperson for the poor and oppressed of society has captured the imaginations of liberation theologians and all those who work for justice. The bishops of Latin America, in the final document of their 1979 Third General Conference in Puebla, *Evangelization at Present and in the Future of Latin America*, express this powerful understanding of Mary as symbol of liberation:

> The *Magnificat* mirrors the soul of Mary. In that canticle we find the culmination of the spirituality of Yahweh's poor and lowly, and of the

prophetic strain in the Old Testament. . . . In the *Magnificat* she presents herself as the model for all those described by Pope John Paul II . . . "who do not passively accept the adverse circumstances of personal and social life. . . ."[9]

Mary is pictured here as an active co-worker in the mission of Jesus. She is seen as a strong and determined woman, who does not allow the many difficulties and discouragements of life to keep her from accomplishing her mission. Mary, by proclaiming the *Magnificat*, is portrayed by the gospel writer as prophetically announcing God's word, that God is on the side of the poor. Truly she is a preacher of the Word! Latin American feminist liberation theologians describe this prophetic role in more female imagery:

> The image of the pregnant woman, able to give birth to the new, is the image of God who through the power

of God's Spirit brings to birth men and women committed to justice, living out their relationship to God in a loving relationship with other human beings.[10]

Mary is regarded here as a powerful image of the God who creates, nurtures, and stands on the side of human beings. This is an image which places a positive value on female bodiliness and sexuality and which stands in sharp contrast to the negativity and suspicion with which women's bodies have often been viewed in Christian tradition.

One problem with past interpretations was that they tended to see Mary, as a model for women only, exemplifying certain "feminine" virtues. Jesus, on the other hand, was the model for men. Both recent biblical studies and the theology of Vatican II support women's calling this into question. Vatican II's theology sees Mary as a type or model for the *whole* church. Her relationship with Jesus is celebrated, not just because of her physical motherhood, but primarily for her role as disciple, who heard the word of God, and kept it. As disciple, Mary is a model for *all* Christians, men as well as women. Likewise, Jesus, in his healing, compassionate ministry, is also imaged by both women and men in their commitment to carry on this ministry in today's world.

Mary is free once again to become our truly human sister, also, because we have realized how sadly impoverished our God-language has been. Although scripture and tradition include both male and female images for God, the almost exclusive reliance on male language, especially father, to describe God has led many to think of God as really being male—an elderly, bearded, white male, for the most part. Traditional Christian theology has always reminded us that God transcends all our attempts to describe the divine reality in human terms, that all our human language falls short. In spite of this, most theological, liturgical, and spiritual traditions have consistently imaged

God in male terms. The intuition that such exclusive use of male images is inadequate to express fully the mystery of God found expression in the past by viewing Mary as at least quasi-divine. The Catholic tradition of devotion to Mary gave us the figure of a woman in whom we could experience and picture divinity.

With the recognition that God's power and liberating action can be disclosed in female as well as male terms comes the liberation of Mary from her role as *the* female image of the divine. Once we are free to call on God as our mother and nurturer as well as father, as gentle, compassionate, *and* just, Mary can be restored to a position firmly on the human side of the divine/human equation. She is disclosive of the divine as model for all human beings who strive to respond in active and creative fidelity to God's action in their lives. Not "alone of all her sex," she is rather a witness to the conviction that all of us bear within ourselves the divine image.

This new approach to Mary, which does not lose sight of the young Jewish woman of the Bible, is also awakening renewed interest on the part of many Protestant Christians, who can accept Mary as sister and example of a life lived by faith in response to grace.

Women are beginning to rediscover and reclaim Mary as sister. She is not the queenly Mary on a pedestal, far out of their reach, nor the romantically demure Mary, the product of male projections, nor the (historically unlikely) blue-eyed blonde who never aged or developed a wrinkle. They claim Mary as a woman who shared the lot of many women, who grew to understand the mission of her child, but was sometimes bewildered by him, a woman who endured homelessness, misunderstanding, and exile; who grew old and likely became a wisdom figure in the early Christian community. The "Litany of Mary of Nazareth," distributed for the Marian Year 1987-1988 by Pax Christi USA, calls on Mary as:

Mother of the homeless,
Widowed mother,
Mother of a political prisoner,
Oppressed woman,
Seeker of sanctuary,
Model of strength,
Model of risk,
First disciple. . . .

This is a new kind of litany arising out of a spirituality that stresses continuities between Mary's life and the lives of many women today. Women today can identify with a Mary who herself is in need of liberation from the past interpretations which so removed her from the experience of other women.

Does this mean we have lost our great intercessor in heaven? Not at all. Mary takes her place as preeminent member of the communion of saints, a traditional Catholic belief witnessing to the strong conviction that the ties that unite us during life as church community are not broken by death. All those who have gone before us (Mary especially) continue to be in solidarity with us who are still on the journey and offer us the hope and the confidence that our lives of faithful discipleship will also be accepted by our loving God.

Questions for Reflection & Discussion

1. *Do the guidelines from* Marialis Cultus *suggest to you ways for renewed public devotion to Mary?*

    Are such public devotions important for your spirituality?

2. *Have the apparitions of Mary played a role in your awareness of her?*

    How can such apparitions be helpful to faith?

    How might they be unhelpful?

3. *What images of God are most powerful for*

you in your life of faith?

4. *Do the insights of liberation theology and feminist theology open up new ways of relating to Mary for you?*

   Which seem to most relate to your experience?

CONCLUSION

Is there a place for Mary in the Christian spirituality of the future? As long as spirituality is not seen as confined to some segmented "religious" dimension of life but as encompassing the whole of life in its ordinary as well as extraordinary moments, there will be a place for Mary. If spirituality means living the whole of life in awareness of the gracious and mysterious presence of God, Mary is a powerful example of a human being whose spiritual journey included doubt, uncertainty, risk, and hope, but who, in the end, proved faithful to God's call and presence in her life. It is time for an older generation of Catholics to rediscover Mary and for a new generation of Christians to meet her. Once again the symbolic figure of Mary, grounded in the biblical picture, may reveal to us the deepest truths about ourselves and about our God. Hopefully, this brief introduction will encourage you to continue on your own journey with Mary.

N O T E S

1. Karl Rahner, "Mary and the Christian Image of Women," *Theological Investigations* XIX, trans. Edward Quinn (Crossroad, 1983), p. 217.

2. Karl Rahner, "The Spirituality of the Church of the Future," *Theological Investigations* XX, trans. Edward Quinn (Crossroad, 1981), p. 147.

3. Walter M Abbott, S.J., ed., *The Documents of Vatican II* (America Press, 1966).

4. John W. Lynch, *A Woman Wrapped in Silence* (Paulist Press, 1968), p. 152.

5. ibid., p. 153.

6. María Clara Bingemer, "Women in the Future of the Theology of Liberation," in *The Future of the Theology of Liberation*, Marc H. Ellis and Otto Maduro, eds., (Orbis Books, 1989).

7. Paul VI, *Marialis Cultus* (USCC, 1974), Introduction.

8. NCCB, *Behold Your Mother* (USCC, 1973), paragraphs 99–100.

9. *Evangelization at Present and in the Future of Latin America* (Puebla) (NCCB, 1979), paragraph 297.

10. Ivone Gebara and María Clara Bingemer, *Mary: Mother of God and Mother of the Poor.* (Orbis Books, 1989), p 73.

SUGGESTIONS FOR
FURTHER READING

Anderson, H. George, et. al., eds. *The One Mediator, the Saints, and Mary*. Lutherans and Catholics in Dialogue VIII. Minneapolis: Augsburg Press, 1992.

Brown, Raymond et al. eds. *Mary in the New Testament*. New York: Paulist Press, 1978.

Brown, R. *The Virginal Conception and the Bodily Resurrection of Jesus*. New York: Paulist Press, 1973.

Coyle, Kathleen. *Mary in the Christian Tradition: From a Contemporary Perspective*. Mystic, CT: Twenty-Third Publications, 1996

Cunneen, Sally. *In Search of Mary: The Woman and the Symbol*. New York: Ballantine Books, 1996.

Donnelly, Doris, ed. *Mary: Woman of Nazareth*. New York: Paulist Press, 1989.

Ebertshauser, Caroline H., et al., eds. *Mary: Art, Culture and Religion through the Ages*. New York: Crossroad, 1998.

Eigo, Francis A., ed. *All Generations Shall Call Me Blessed*. Villanova: Villanova University Press, 1994.

Hines, Mary E. "Mary" in T*he New Dictionary of Catholic Spirituality*, Michael Downey, ed. 635-645. Collegeville: Liturgical Press, 1993.

Jegen, Carol. *Mary according to Women*. Kansas City: Leaven Press, 1985.

John Paul II. "Homily at the Shrine of Our Lady of Guadalupe," Jan. 27, 1979. In Origins 8, no. 34 (Feb. 8, 1979): 539-41.

John Paul II. *The Mother of the Redeemer.* Washington, D.C.: USCC, 1987

Johnson, Ann. *Miryam of Nazareth: Woman of Strength and Wisdom.* Notre Dame, IN: Ave Maria Press, 1984.

Johnson, Elizabeth. *"The Marian Tradition and the Reality of Women." Horizons* 12 (1985), 116-135.

Laurentin, René. *The Apparitions of the Blessed Virgin Mary Today.* Dublin: Veritas, 1990.

Pelikan, Jaroslav. *Mary through the Centuries*. New Haven: Yale University Press, 1996.

Rahner, Karl. *Mary: Mother of the Lord.* Wheathampstead Hertfordshire: Anthony Clarke Books, 1963.

Rodriguez, Jeanette. *Our Lady of Guadalupe.* Austin: University of Texas Press, 1994.

Ruether, Rosemary. *Mary: The Feminine Face of the Church.* Philadelphia: Westminster, 1977.

Tambasco, Anthony. *What Are They Saying about Mary?* New York: Paulist Press, 1984.

Tavard, George. *The Thousand Faces of the Virgin Mary.* Collegeville MN: Liturgical Press, 1996.

Vatican II, *Constitution on the Church* (*Lumen Gentium*). Chapters 7 and 8.

Warner, Marina. *Alone of All Her Sex.* London: Picador, 1976.

Zimdars-Swartz, Sandra. *Encountering Mary: From LaSalette to Medjugorje.* Princeton, NJ: Princeton University Press, 1991.

MARY E. HINES is Professor of Theology at Emmanuel College in Boston, Massachusetts. She has written extensively on the topic of Mary following Vatican II, as well as on ministry and the church. She is a member of many professional theological societies, and has held offices in the Catholic Theological Society of America.